How To Prepare A Profitable Strategic Business Plan

John Millar

ISBN:154053345X
ISBN-13:9781540533456

DEDICATION

I dedicate this book to my mother and father, who
raised me while self-employed. They
taught me to work hard and listen to everyone but to
make my own choices as to what is right
and what is wrong.. and oh, did I mention work hard?

Anyone who tells you to work smart not hard hasn't
ever done it tough and realized that if
you work smart AND hard you will achieve more than
you can possibly dream.

CONTENTS

About This Program   7

1   Strategic Business Planning – Defined   9

2   Strategic Business Planning – A Simplistic Overview   11

3   Task 1 - Define The Business / Develop A Vision   25

4   Task 2 - Setting Of Strategic Business Objectives / Factors   45

5   Task 3 - Developing Smart Strategic Action Plans   58

6   Summary   63

7   About the author   66

8   Testimonials   68

STRATEGIC BUSINESS PLANNING – DEFINED

Strategic business planning involves the organization's (a strategic business unit, division, region, country, facility, product team, sales team, department…) attempt to spell out in clear detail the paths by which the organization's vision is to be accomplished and how progress toward that vision will be measured and tracked. This process defines success in the context of the business the organization wants to be in, how success in that business will be quantified, what will be done to achieve it, what resources (time, money, people, products, technology…) will be required, and what kind of organizational culture is necessary to achieve this success — while remaining consistent with the overall mission of the corporation.

Briefly, strategic business planning produces a quantified version of the organization's desired

future.

In this process, the planning team is asked to conceptualize a series of specific future scenarios and then to decide which of these futures they wish to pursue and create. Strategic business planning is a chance for the planning team to develop and shape its vision for an ideal future before getting down to the nuts and bolts of figuring out how to reach that future, what will be required, and who will be responsible.

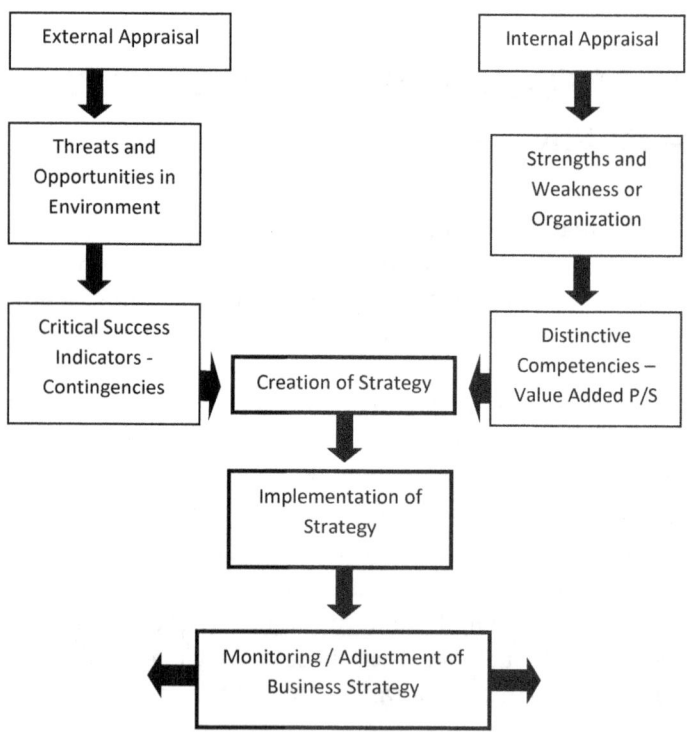

STRATEGIC BUSINESS PLANNING – A SIMPLISTIC OVERVIEW

Just the name "Strategic Business Planning" can be intimidating on its own, but then add in the hodge-podge of complex processes and arcane terminology and the whole thing can become quite messy. Therefore, we thought it might be helpful to give a sort of watered-down and simplistic overview of what the strategic planning process really represents at a business level.

1. Create a clear, vivid, compelling vision for the future of the business. Where do you want your team to be in 3-5 years. This needs to be detailed, specific, and realistic – but challenging. If you are planning for a division or region – your vision must be congruent with the overall vision and business plan for the corporation. Your plans, goals and targets – must roll-up effectively

to the corporate plans — and especially those of your direct supervisors.

2.   Once you get a clear idea of where you want to take your business – you'll need to do a VERY in-depth analysis of all of the various factors that will impact your ability to achieve the vision you have set forth. This sort of research and number crunching is exhaustive, detailed, and difficult work – but it must be done completely and thoroughly if the plan is to be effective.

3.   After completing all of the research and analysis — you can go back and take a look at your vision to determine if it is still realistic and viable. Based on your conclusions, the next step is to identify the most important areas to focus your efforts (Strategic Business Objectives) – where to allocate time, money, people and resources for the greatest competitive impact. Also, you will uncover critical areas of concern that must be monitored as potential threats to the successful implementation of your plan and create contingencies should they occur.

4.   Implementation and monitoring of the plan is where the rubber meets the road – where dreams turn into work. You will set out specific, measurable, agreed upon and time-bound goals to achieve the vision – and take action on them. Assessing results, tracking numbers, coaching and motivating to stay on plan.

5.   The last step takes you back to the first. Evaluate the effectiveness and success of the plan (every six months or year). Re-adjust the vision if required and begin the process over again. Strategic business

planning is a process – there is never a time when the plan is complete, it simply keeps getting extended out additional years.

WHAT IS STRATEGIC PLANNING?

LONG-TERM IMPACT OF CURRENT DECISIONS

First, planning deals with the future impact of current decisions. This means that strategic planning looks at the chain of cause and effect consequences over time of an actual or intended decision that a manager is going to make. If the manager does not like what is seen ahead, the decision can be readily changed before resources are committed. Strategic business planning also looks at the alternative courses of action that are open in the future, and how those various choices influence decisions being made today.

The essence of formal strategic business planning is the systematic identification of opportunities and threats that lie in the future, which in combination with other relevant data provide a basis for a company's making better current decisions to exploit the opportunities and avoid the threats.

PROCESS

Second, strategic planning is a process. It is a process that begins with the setting of organizational aims and vision, defines strategies and policies to achieve them, and develops detailed plans to make sure that the strategies are implemented so as to achieve the ends sought. It is a process of deciding in advance what kind of planning effort is to be undertaken, who is going to do it, how it is done, and what will be done with the results. It is an on-going process that continues to cycle forward, extending out for the life of the company.

PHILOSOPHY

Third, strategic planning is an attitude, a way of life. Planning necessitates dedication to acting in the basis of contemplation of the future, a determination to plan constantly and systematically as an integral part of organizational management and a key element in the culture of the company.

STRUCTURE

Fourth, a formal strategic planning system links together the three major types of planning:

- Long-term (3-10 year) Strategic Plans
- Medium-range (6 to 36 month) Program Plans
- Short-range (1 –24 month) Budgets and Operational / Tactical Implementation Plans

WHAT STRATEGIC PLANNING IS NOT!

Strategic planning does not attempt to make future decisions. Forward planning requires that choices be made among possible events in the future, but decisions made in their light can be made only in the present.

Strategic planning is not forecasting product sales and then determining what should be done to assure the fulfillment of the forecasts with respect to such things as materials purchases, facilities, manpower, and so on. Strategic planning goes far beyond forecasts of current markets and products and asks the more fundamental questions: Are we in the right business? What are our basic objectives? When will our present products become obsolete? Are our markets accelerating or eroding? For most companies there is a wide gap between an objective forecasting of present sales and profits and what top management would like sales and profits to be. If so, that is a gap to be filled by strategic planning.

Strategic Planning is not an attempt to blueprint the future. It is not the development of a set of plans that are cast in stone - to be used day after day without change into the distant future. Good strategic plans are flexible, responsive and adaptable.

Strategic planning is not necessarily the preparation of massive, detailed, and interrelated sets of plans. It can range from the very simple - to the highly complex.

Strategic planning is not an attempt to replace good managerial judgment. Strategic planning is carried out in order to assist in making sound business decisions – that are congruent with the direction of the overall corporate mission, vision and strategic plan.

Strategic planning is not simply an aggregation of functional plans or an extrapolation of current budgets. It is truly a systematic approach to maneuvering an enterprise over time through the uncertain waters of its changing environment to achieve prescribed organizational objectives. Strategic planning is about proactively creating the future of the enterprise, not figuring out where the company will be based on a long-term trend analysis of current numbers.

WHY STRATEGIC PLANNING PAYS OFF

ASKS AND ANSWERS QUESTIONS OF IMPORTANCE

For top managers, as well as for all other managers in an organization, formal strategic planning asks and answers some key questions in an orderly way, with a scale of priority and urgency. Such questions as the following come to mind: What is our basic line of business? What are our underlying philosophies and purpose? What are the company's long-range and short-range goals? What and where are our markets? What will our cash flow be over the next several years? How will we remain competitive? What sort of skills and talent will we need? How should we invest current funds back into the company to secure the future of the venture? Where is our industry headed? — and many, many more.

SIMULATES THE FUTURE

One of the great advantages of strategic planning is that it simulates the future - on paper. If the situation does not result in the desired picture the exercise can be erased and started all over again. Simulation exercises are reversible - so no brick and mortar or banking decisions are made without the careful examination of the future.

FORCES THE SETTING OF BUSINESS OBJECTIVES

A strategic planning process will not get very far if at

some point specific objectives are not set for such things as sales, profits and market share. There is no doubt that individuals will generally strive hard to achieve clear objectives that are set for their organization.

FRAMEWORK FOR DECISION MAKING

One of the more important attributes of an effective planning program is that it gives clear and specific guidance to managers throughout a business as to priorities and objectives that are in line with the aims and strategies of upper management.

PERFORMANCE MEASUREMENT

A comprehensive plan provides the basis for measuring performance. Management has available standards of both a qualitative and a quantitative nature in a strategic plan.

CHANNEL OF COMMUNICATION

A well-organized planning system is an extremely useful communications tool. The planning process is a means for communicating among all levels of management about objectives, strategies, and detailed operational plans. Strategic plans form the basis of Management By Objectives, delegation, accountability, empowerment and team work.

VARIED GOALS FOR STRATEGIC BUSINESS PLANNING

1. Change the direction of the company / division / team.

2. Accelerate growth and improve profitability.

3. Uncover strategic issues for top management consideration.

4. Concentrate resources on important areas - allocate assets to areas of best potential.

5. Develop better information for managers to make sound decisions.

6. Develop a frame of reference for budgets and short-range operating plans.

7. Develop situation analysis of opportunities and threats to provide better awareness of a company's potential in light of its strengths and weaknesses.

8. Increase coordination of internal activities.

9. Develop superb communications within the organization.

10. Gain more control of operations.

11. Develop a sense of security among managers coming from an improved understanding of changing environment and the company's ability to adapt to it.

12. Provide a road map to show where the

company is going and how to get there.

13. Setting more realistic, demanding, yet attainable objectives.

14. Review and audit current operations so as to make proper adjustments and modifications as a result of changing environmental and organizational factors.
15. Provide awareness of changing environment in order to better adapt to it.

16. Pick up the pace of a "tired" company.

5 TASKS OF STRATEGIC BUSINESS PLANNING

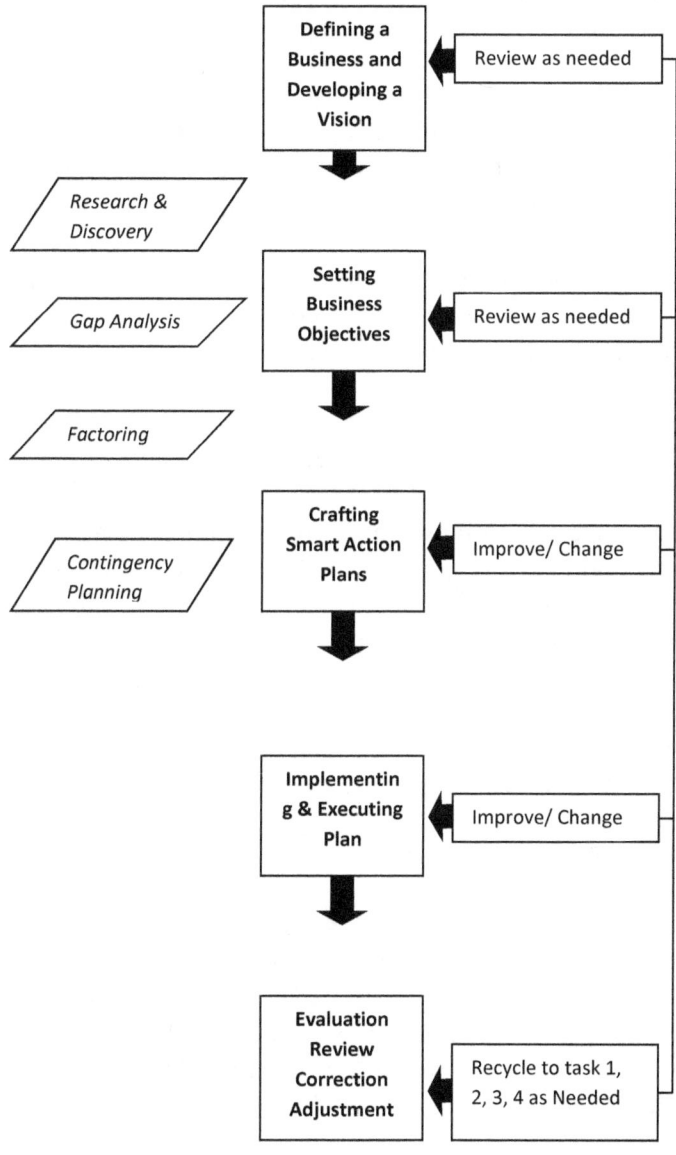

BEFORE STRATEGIC BUSINESS PLANNING – BUSINESS THINKING

There is a wonderful book called *Business Think* written by the folks at Franklin Covey that puts forward an excellent framework for good, solid strategic thinking when making important business decisions. Rater than try to reinvent the wheel – here my version of their wheel that already runs very smoothly (I would also highly recommend buying the book — if you think this short list is good– you should see the rest of the book!).

1. CHECK YOUR EGO AT THE DOOR

Arrogance, defensiveness, the desperate need for approval and the fight to feel like a winner (and make the other person feel like a loser) shut down dialogue, opportunities and decisions and end up devouring time and energy, not to mention people. Changing yourself, changing your mindset, changing your behaviors and attitudes — can lead to changing the business (and your life). Stay focused on your purpose: the best solution.

2. CREATE CURIOSITY

Curiosity is the driving force behind Business Thinking, and it thrives on intellectual diversity. Breakthrough solutions require fresh thinking, and curiosity drives your exploration of the unknown. What we currently know can get in the way of the unknown and the pursuit of phenomenal solutions and strategies.

Your ability to enact curiosity can help create a culture that encourages everyone to ask questions and discourages those who don't.

It ain't what you don't know that will hurt

you...

It's what you do know – that ain't so!

3. MOVE OFF THE SOLUTION

Solutions are only valuable for the results they get – and some solutions are better than others. Avoid solutions that serve more as a distraction than as bona fide solutions. Get to the core of the underlying business issues that need to be addressed – by moving past the easy answers and focusing on bringing clarity and definition to the issue – then deciding to give attention to the few solutions that truly meet your business needs and requirements.

Look for the second (or third) correct answer.

4. GET EVIDENCE

If you don't have evidence, there is no reason to do anything – **period!** Get proof that a business problem needs to be solved or that an opportunity *could* exist - by collecting soft evidence, and then converting soft evidence into hard evidence that your business can measure. It is important to achieve a high confidence level in the soundness of your evidence and assumptions based on those facts.

5.   CALCULATE THE IMPACT

Just because you *can* do something – does not mean you *should*. It is not unusual that the cost of a solution is more expensive then the cost of living with the problem. Make sure early on that your solution has a worthwhile impact on the company, and a solid economic return. You'll never know unless you convert hard evidence into monetary impact – this will help you move from the subjective to the objective and from the *could*, to the *should*.

6.   EXPLORE THE RIPPLE EFFECT

By widening your functional lens to capture the broader impact of problems or opportunities on the company, you are calculating more than financial impact. Make sure you know who or what else in the company is affected to get the full scope of the impact.

7.   SLOW DOWN FOR YELLOW LIGHTS

There are hurdles that can stop any solution in it's tracks. If the problem or opportunity is a big as you think it is, what stopped everyone from successfully doing anything about it before now? What (or who) might stop you in the future?

It is impossible to build an effective strategic business plan, without the proper strategic mind set and thinking skills.

TASK 1 - DEFINE THE BUSINESS / DEVELOP A VISION

The foremost direction-setting question managers of any enterprise need to ask is: **"What is our business and what will it be?"** Developing a carefully reasoned answer to this question pushes managers to consider what the organization's business makeup should be and to develop a clearer vision of where the organization needs to be headed over the next 3-5 years. Management's answer to **"What is our business and what will it be?"** begins the process of carving out a meaningful direction for the organization to take and establishing a strong organizational identity. Sometimes called either a Mission Statement or a Vision Statement, there are five key questions to consider when developing this important tool.

DEFINING THE DIMENSIONS OF A VISION

1. *What is the thrust or focus for future business development?*
2. *What is the scope of products and markets that will - and will NOT - be considered.*
3. *What is the future emphasis or priority and mix for the products and markets that fall within that scope?*
4. *What key capabilities / resources are required to make this strategic Vision happen? (money, products, people, equipment, technology, sales, advertising, distribution, service, support...)*
5. *What does this Vision imply for growth and return expectations?*

It is critical to develop a clear, specific, measurable and desirable vision for the business. This is the cornerstone to motivation, delegation and effective implementation of the plan. The leader must be able to vividly articulate and analytically describe the scope, direction, focus and future of the organization.

> *** Key point : Remember - the ultimate mission of any company is always to serve the customer.**

WHAT IS THE VISION FOR YOUR BUSINESS

In the following exercise we are going to work on creating a vision statement for your company, business division or team. This will be the target you set for you and your organization to shoot for - the future you want to create. The time frame will be 3-5 years. Don't get to hung up on making it sound grand or eloquent – what is important is that it clearly describes who you want to be, what it will look like, and how it will be measured on key indicators like revenue, number of customers served, market share and such. Here are some questions to think about as you formulate your vision:

Who is our customer now – who will it be in the future – what will they want? What is our business now and what will it be in 5 years (specifically)?

How does this fit with the overall organization's vision and strategic plan?

What markets will we try to compete in? What markets or customers will we abandon? Who will we be competing against and how will we be positioned in relation to them? How do we want the public to think of our company, products and services?

What are our core corporate values that will carry us there?

How will we treat our employees – retain top talent and attract new key people? What will our key numbers be? By what date?

Here is a basic example for a mid-sized advertising agency:

"In 2007, Adbiz will be a highly regarded, creative and award-winning agency that delivers superior products and services to our clients through a world class staff of creative, focused — yet fun — advertising and marketing professionals. Working from our new corporate headquarters in Alachua, Florida, we will have a staff of almost 100 amazing people and will be recognized as one of the top 50 agencies in the United States, generating total revenue of more than 70 million from major national accounts and selected smaller target accounts..."

This might then be backed up with a list of key financial and market numbers that would.

Specifically, identify the business revenue targets for the organization.

VISION STATEMENT - THINK SHEET

It may help in creating your Vision if you can put some specific detail as to what you want your business to look like in the future.

In ____ years, our company (division / team) will...

Have gross revenues of _____

A net profit % of _____

Total number of employees _____

Our product mix will be _____

We will be unique and valuable in the marketplace because _____
_____

Our main customer base will be
_____

Our major competitors will be
_____

Our corporate culture will be
_____

We will NOT
_____

Additional comments:

VISION STATEMENT – WORKSHOP

Use the space below to begin the first draft of a vision statement for your business. If you already have a vision statement - reflect on the answers you gave on part one of the exercise and determine if your statement is still on track - or if it may need some adjustment.

_____

_____
_____
_____
_____
_____
_____
_____
_____
_____
_____
_____
_____
_____
_____
_____
_____
_____
_____
_____
_____
_____
_____

GAP ANALYSIS

Now that you have developed a clear and specific idea as to where you want to take your organization over the next 3-5 years - the next assignment is to step back and take a very close look at exactly where you are today via a performance audit. The difference between where you want to go – *your vision* – and where you are at this moment in time is called the "Gap."

A Gap Analysis refers to an in-depth audit of data - past /present / future - that provides a base for pursuing the strategic planning process. Typical activities covered in this analysis include the current performance appraisal, situation audit, SWOT analysis, competitive analysis, the market/business audit, or the planning premises. These processes are designed to give the company a realistic and thorough overview of the starting place for the strategic plan.

The major objective of the gap analysis is to identify and analyze the key trends, and phenomena having a potential impact on the formulation and implementation of strategies for achieving your vision. This is a critical planning step for two reasons:

First, there are changes in the environment of a business that will have a profound impact on the affairs of the enterprise. Best results will be achieved if these forces are identified *before* the impact is felt, in contrast to attempting to react to foreseeable market shifts.

Second, the results of conducting a gap analysis

often lead to an enhanced understanding of current business processes - helping to identify and prioritize key areas of change.

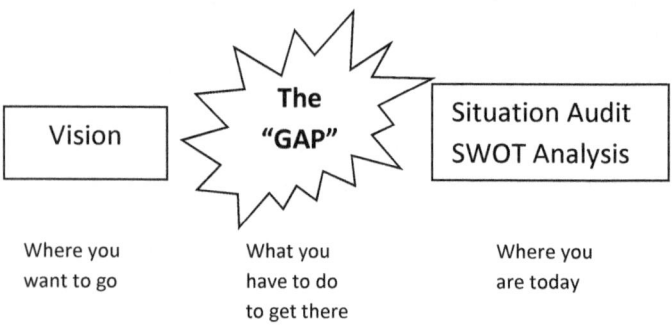

Vision	The "GAP"	Situation Audit SWOT Analysis
Where you want to go	What you have to do to get there	Where you are today

SWOT ANALYSIS – WHICH LEADS TO YOUR GAP

The SWOT (strengths, weaknesses, opportunities, threats) analysis is a concerted effort to realistically and honestly determine where the business is today – so that you can make a direct comparison to the desired vision and determine exactly what must be done to close the gap between the two positions. The SWOT analysis involves an in-depth, simultaneous study of both the organization's internal strengths and weaknesses and those significant factors (opportunities and threats) outside the organization that may positively of negatively impact its future. A realistic appraisal of where the organization currently stands in these terms is the crux of a viable performance appraisal and the very foundation of an effective strategic business plan.

Internal Strengths and Weaknesses

The purpose of this phase of the planning process is to identify those areas of weakness that must be managed, improved or avoided, as well as identifying areas for focus and investment where the business has superior strengths or unique opportunities for success. Many organization have great difficulty effectively assessing the internal weaknesses of their business, as no one likes to focus on the negative and there may be a good bit of fear in uncovering serious problems in operations or people. However, without a *brutally honest* assessment of these areas of weakness – it puts the organization in great jeopardy. It is imperative that the internal performance analysis be done with equal scrutiny to both strengths and weaknesses.

External Opportunities and Threats

The performance audit must also include information about the outside forces that may impact the organization's goals. These outside forces are considered the opportunities and threats of the SWOT analysis. The planning team must study competitors, suppliers, markets and customers, economic trends, labor-market conditions and government regulations on all levels that can affect the organization positively or negatively. This analysis should include both current and future trends – a longitudinal study.

When conducting the SWOT analysis it is important to include the following environments:

1. The general business / social / economic environment
2. Your unique industry environment
3. Your organization-specific environment
4. The competitive environment

SWOT ANALYSIS – WORKSHOP

On the following pages you will be asked a myriad of questions regarding to the current status of your business to get you thinking. Do your best to answer the questions when possible - however if you simply do not know the answer - put a large question mark next to it. This will be a signal that you need to find an answer for that question at a later date.

(Answer on a separate sheet)

CUSTOMERS
- What markets do we now serve?
- What new market should we serve?
- What is our profitability?
- What part of the business should we be getting out of?
- What is the required investment (time, money, people) to serve our customers?
- How do our customers view us?
- What do they think we do well or poorly?
- What is our level of repeat customers / churn / growth?

COMPETITION
- Who are our major three direct competitors?

- How are we viewed in comparison to our major competitors?
- What is their marketing / competitive strategy? Level of aggressiveness?
- What advantages do they have over us? Can we attack them?
- What are our advantages over them? Can we defend against them?
- What other P/S might be considered competitive or a replacement?

PRODUCTS/SERVICES (P/S)

- What are the specific P/S for which our customers come to us?
- What are the most distinctive P/S we offer?
- What are the new P/S vs. the fading P/S?
- How do our P/S compare with competitors? How can we differentiate our offerings?
- What economic (value added) factors do we provide? Do our customers believe them?
- What are the most profitable P/S we offer - the least?

SWOT ANALYSIS - WORKSHOP

PRICES

- How are our prices set? How much flexibility do we have? When were they last reviewed?
- How do they compare competitively?
- Are we meeting our targets for profitability and market share?

FACILITIES (PLANT AND EQUIPMENT)

- Do we have the facilities / equipment / technology we need? Do we know what is available in the industry?
- Do we have controls over productivity? Obsolescence?
- Are we dependent on other companies for our manufacturing process / services? Do we manage our value chain effectively?

FINANCES

- What is our flexibility for growth? For recession?
- What sources of funds do we use? Are there other sources we can tap in to? What risks are we exposed to? What is the worst-case scenario?
- What controls do we have over cash, receivables, inventories, debt? What controls should we have?

DECISION MAKING

- What decisions are critical to our business? Who makes those decisions?
- Are those decisions based on adequate information? Is the information reliable? Are the decisions made in a timely fashion?
- Are the decisions reviewed later for effectiveness ?
- Are people held accountable for their decisions

and actions?

- Are people rewarded or punished for bold decision making? For making mistakes? How can our decision making be improved? Making? For making mistakes? How can our decision making be improved?

SWOT ANALYSIS – WORKSHOP

PROFITABILITY

- How do we compare with the industry?
- How do we currently compare to our best period?
- Are there P/S that we can provide and charge a premium for?
- Can we renegotiate with our suppliers to reduce our COGS?
- Can we slow down our accounts payable?
- Can we speed up our accounts receivables?
- Are we often trapped into discounting? If so why?
- Can we reduce inventory to free-up cash?

PEOPLE

- What do we know about our current management and technical staff in terms of: - *age, skills, potential, turnover, and retirement*?
- How does our salary/benefit program compare with the industry standard?
- What are the expectations of our staff?
- Do we have enough staff to handle

current/future work? Too many?
- What is our process for building the skills of our staff?
- What is our corporate culture?
- How do our people feel about the company?
- How do they feel about the future of the company?

DANGERS

What changes that could occur would have a significant impact on:
- products and services
- customers
- markets
- key staff
- location
- sources of supply
- competitors
- regulatory/legal environment
- finances/economy

SWOT ANALYSIS

- STRENGTHS / WEAKNESSES / OPPORTUNITIES / THREATS

POTENTIAL INTERNAL STRENGTHS

- Core competencies in key areas
- Adequate financial resources
- Well thought of by customers

- Insulated from strong competitive pressure
- Proprietary technology / data
- Cost advantages
- Superior advertising
- Product innovation skills
- Superior manufacturing capability
- Ahead on experience curve
- Proven management
- Key people / talent / knowledge

POTENTIAL INTERNAL WEAKNESSES

- No clear strategic direction
- Obsolete facilities
- Subpar profitability
- Lack of management depth / talent
- Missing key skills / competencies
- Poor track record in implementing strategy
- Falling behind in R&D
- Too narrow a product line
- Weak market image
- Below average marketing skills
- Unable to finance needed changes
- Higher COGS than competitors
- Internal strife / corporate in-fighting

POTENTIAL EXTERNAL OPPORTUNITIES

- Additional customer groups
- New markets / segments
- Expand product line
- Diversify into related markets

- Vertical integration (forward / backward)
- Complacency among rival firms
- Faster market growth
- Demographic trends
- Future technology
- Regulatory changes
- Economic shifts

POTENTIAL EXTERNAL THREATS

- Entry of competitors
- Rising sale of substitute products
- Slower market growth
- Adverse shift in regulations
- Vulnerability to recession and business cycle
- Growing bargaining power of suppliers and customers
- Changing buyer needs and tastes
- Adverse demographic changes
- Bad press / publicity

SWOT ANALYSIS - WORKSHOP

TOP 5 INTERNAL STRENGTHS

_____

_____

_____

_____

_____

_____

_____

TOP 5 INTERNAL WEAKNESSES

_____

_____

_____

_____

_____

TOP 5 EXTERNAL OPPORTUNITIES

_____

_____

_____

TOP 5 EXTERNAL THREATS

SWOT ANALYSIS – ADDITIONAL TOOLS

Some additional analysis tools for conducting a thorough SWOT analysis might include:

Competitive Benchmarking: taking a close look at your competitors on a number of key indicators (price, customer service ratings, product offerings, value-added services) and using their measures as a target or "benchmark" for your planning goals.

Best-in-class Benchmarking: looking at the leading organizations in a specific type of measure and using their measures as your key target measures (for example looking at the Ritz Carlton or Disney for customer service measurements).

Competitive Positioning: creating a chart that visually depicts you position in the total marketplace compared to your leading competitors on key indicators such as price, customer service, technology, market share.

MECE: based on a technique used by the consultant of McKinsey & Company, this stands for Mutually Exclusive – Comprehensively Exhaustive. Assign two separate planning teams to attack the same issue. Instruct them to work independently and to be extremely thorough. Then compare their findings and recommendations – for overlap, inconsistencies, common themes and contradictory views.

Tactics for Closing the Gap

1. Lengthen time for accomplishing the vision: This tactic should be considered if the current allocation of resources is appropriate – but it will take more time than anticipated to reach a set of aggressive strategic goals.

2. Reduce the size or scope of the vision: When there is not enough resources – or the vision is deemed to risky.

3. Reallocate resources to achieve the goals: the vision is appropriate but additional resources will be needed to make the time table or eliminate undue risk.

4. Obtain new resources: when new talent, products, markets, capital, technology are necessary to achieve the vision.

5. Retrenchment: when downsizing, divestiture or shutting down all or part of a business is necessary to reduce risk and fee up resources in an effort to achieve the vision.

TASK 2 - SETTING OF STRATEGIC BUSINESS OBJECTIVES / FACTORS

The next step in the strategic planning process is to identify all of the various elements that need to be addressed in the plan - then set clear and specific objectives and action steps to achieve the vision.

The tool we use to bring order to the chaos we have just created in the SWOT analysis is factoring.

DEFINITION: A Factor is a clear statement of fact about anything that could positively of negatively affect our ability to achieve the Vision.

Factoring is a process of identifying everything that

could help or hurt us in our quest to create our future vision of the company. Factors are always written as a complete sentence - and as a statement of fact. It may be that you simply go in and assign factoring priorities to some of your existing information from the SWOT analysis — but you may also need to write out a good number of specific factors based on the information you have developed.

Factors must be clear, easy to understand, specific statements about what you know and do not know about your current and future situations. A typical strategic plan will have dozens or hundreds of unique factors – so be sure to number every factor so that you can track and cross-reference each of them later.

Examples:

1. We Know that our major competitors are Acme and Ajax.
2. We currently have 15% market share.
3. We Don't Know (DK) if Sun Systems is planning to enter our market.
4. We DK if we can renegotiate our supplier contracts.
5. We DK if we can automate part of our production process.
6. We Know that our current computer system is not sufficient for our needs.
7. We DK the technical specifications of an acceptable computer system.

After you have written out your factors - go back and prioritize all of them using the following criteria:

A = Very Important - take immediate action.
B = Important - action required (may be dependent on another factor).
C = Important - but no action required (information to keep in mind).

The first place to start your factoring process is to go back and look over the information you compiled in the SWOT analysis. You should have a long list of questions and answers - many of your factors will come from this list. Remember, if you could not answer a question you put a question mark (?) next to it - these now all become DK's for your factoring list.

To aid in creating a very complete factor list, utilize the following factor categories to help generate even more ideas.

FINANCIAL
Gross revenues / profits Sales
Debt Cash flow
Retained Earnings Credit
A/P and A/R Bad debt Shrinkage Obsolete stock

RESOURCE EFFICIENCY
Sales per employee
Profits per employee
Investment per employee
Use of employee skills
Economies of scale
Collective purchasing
Vertical integration

Process reengineering
Value-chain management
Cycle Time Automation

EMPLOYEES
Skills, abilities, competencies, attitudes Productivity
Turnover
Diversity
Training Corporate culture Benefits

FACILITIES
Capacity
Modernization
Location
Appearance
Cost

MARKETING
Markets served
New markets
Markets to exit
Niche markets
Market share
Demographic and psychographic trends
Targeted and consistent marketing message
Marketing channels

FACTORS WORKSHEET

Factoring is basically a data-dump of all relevant information — *stated clearly and factually – and then prioritized (A,B,C)* — about everything you'll need to keep in mind as you begin to formulate your overall strategy. Look over all of the answers from your SWOT analysis and write at least 10 specific factors on business critical issues that you must focus on when creating your plan.

_____
_____
_____
_____
_____
_____
_____
_____
_____
_____
_____
_____
_____
_____

Once you have completed the factoring process, you should have a very long and comprehensive list of prioritized factors. The next step is to group your factors into main categories to uncover trends. As you look at your factors list, some groupings will be quite obvious - others may only contain a single factor.

Some examples might be:

Sales	Products
Marketing	Competition
Suppliers	Customers
Employees	Technology
Finances	Region
Facilities	Production

The aim here is to find a handful of similar factors that constitute a focus of organizational effort. These will become your major business objectives (your corporate strategy) for the next 3-5 years – . Once you have identified a group, closely examine the focus and direction of the similar factors and then develop a broad "Strategic Business Objective" category (also referred to as a *Strategic Thrust*) -that encompasses all the related factors.

Example: You may currently have a poor marketing / advertising program, and some of the factors might be:

1. We are not well known in the community. A
2. We DK exactly how we are viewed by the general public. A
3. We have 5,000 brochures left from the last printing. C
4. Our advertising budget for this year is $100,000. B
5. We DK the best way to reach our target market. A

Based on these factors - AND - our long-term vision statement - you might create a strategic business objective that states:

Objective 4 : Create a targeted, 2-year marketing campaign to position ABC Inc. as the innovative solution provider for small business printing needs in the Jacksonville market.

> ** After you have grouped all of your factors and developed a focused list of long-range strategic business objectives - prioritize that list from the most important (mission critical) to the least important. This list now constitutes the framework of your business strategy – how you will close the gap and achieve your

WHAT IS STRATEGY?

OPERATIONAL EFFECTIVENESS IS NOT STRATEGY

Companies must be flexible to respond rapidly to competitive and market changes. They must benchmark continuously to achieve best practice. They must outsource aggressively to gain efficiencies. And must nurture and grow a few core competencies to stay ahead of rivals.

The root of the problem however, is the failure to distinguish between truly competitive and defendable strategies — and the simple focus for improved operational effectiveness. The quest for productivity, quality, and speed has spawned a remarkable number of management tools and techniques: TQM, Six Sigma, ISO 9000, Value Chain Management, JIT inventory, theory of constraints, time-based competition, strategic outsourcing, strategic alliances, partnering. Although the resulting operational improvements from these programs have often been dramatic, many companies have been frustrated in their inability to sustain and true competitive advantage or profitability from these initiatives.

OPERATIONAL EFFECTIVENESS: NECESSARY – BUT NOT SUFFICIENT

Cost is generated by performing activities –

manufacturing a product, developing software code, recording data, delivering services, managing information and people. Cost advantage arises from performing those activities more efficiently than competitors. Similarly, cost differentiations and advantages also arise from both the *choices of activities to be performed and how those activities are performed.* Activities then, are the basic building blocks of competitive advantage. Over all advantage or disadvantage in the marketplace results from the totality of a company's activities.

OPERATIONAL EFFECTIVENESS VS. STRATEGIC DIFFERENTIATION

Operational Effectiveness (OE) means performing similar activities better than the competition performs them. Operational effectiveness includes, but is not limited to efficiency. OE basically means to do the same activities as your competitor — just to do them faster, better, cheaper. In contrast, strategic differentiation means doing different activities, or the same activities in completely different ways. A strategy based on OE is much more easily copied – where as a strategy based on unique and defendable differentiation is much more difficult to replicate and effectively compete against.

> **STRATEGY RESTS ON UNIQUE ACTIVITIES: THE ESSENCE OF STRATEGY IS CHOOSING TO PERFORM ACTIVITIES DIFFERENTLY - OR DIFFERENT ACTIVITIES — THAN RIVALS DO.**

WHAT MAKES A TRULY COMPETITIVE STRATEGY?

FIRST, IS IT UNIQUE?

Does it reflect a powerful business model; do something that's unequivocally world-class, best-of-breed, special, different, and fun (yes...fun)? Is it so unique and special that it intrigues, excites, even dazzles customers and staff? And, does it clearly offer value in the market place? In other words, in addition to being cool, cutting edge and brilliant – people are interested, excited, motivated... almost demanding to pay lots of money for it.

That is what a good business strategy is supposed to do!

SECOND, IS THE STRATEGY COHERENT?

Does it generate clarity, commitment and consensus among employees as to the priorities and values of the organization? Does it create an exciting vision of the future of the organization that people want to get involved with, know exactly where the business is going and are motivated to dedicate a part of their life to helping it get there?

THIRD, IS IT DELIVERABLE?

A great idea is worthless without execution. Can you take this business dream – and make it a business reality. Will you be able to implement, measure and hold people accountable for the execution of your strategy? Will your strategy work in the real world?

Which leads me to…

LASTLY, IS THE STRATEGY EVER-EVOLVING?

Does the company have a process in place to ensure that the priorities, goals, objective and values put forth in the strategy do not stagnate. That they are constantly measured, tested, talked about, debated and improved. *This is not a once a year deal – it is an everyday deal.* Why? People have a short memory – you have to keep them focused on the goal, focused on your values, focused on a clear, specific, vivid and compelling vision of the organization and a realistic strategy that clearly spells out in great detail exactly what you are trying to achieve and each person's interdependent role in making it happen.

> *Before you set your strategic business objectives — make sure that they create a truly competitive business strategy.*

THE VALUE NET

When forming a strategy – it is crucial to keep in mind the different dimensions on which a successful strategist can deploy unique objectives. All of these areas represent opportunities for creating differentiation and establishing competitive advantage.

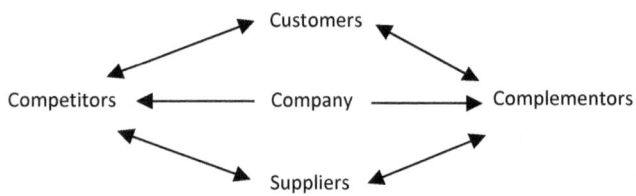

MAKING STRATEGIC DECISIONS

Delay in making critical strategic decisions can be costly – missed opportunities, lost market share, first-mover advantage... But decisions made too hastily can also cause significant damage. How do you make these key strategic decisions in a timely and confident fashion?

ASK FOR HELP

Ask questions, do research, gather data, look at trends – anything to collect reliable information that is pertinent to the decision – in a reasonable time frame. As the old saying goes: "chance favors the prepared mind."

POTENTIAL IMPACT

The technique to look at the long-term potential impact of the decision and invest a level of time and effort in decision making that is appropriate to the scope of the problem.

Building a new factory requires huge invest of time, capital and people – and should drive a significant amount of planning and careful decision making. Deciding what color t-shirts to buy for the annual picnic does not have the same level of potential impact, so that decision should be made with very little investment of time or effort.

TASK 2 - SETTING BUSINESS OBJECTIVES – STRATEGIC THRUSTS

List a major business objective below – with all of the related factors below it.

TASK 3 - DEVELOPING SMART STRATEGIC ACTION PLANS

Once you have completed the factoring process - and have prioritized all of your strategic business objectives - it is time to take the each of these objectives and their related factors and create a set of Specific, Measurable, Agreed upon, Realistic, and Time-bound (SMART) action steps to achieve the objective.

In order of priority, take each of the factors and decide specifically what needs to be done - by who - by when.

For example: Under a strategic objective dealing with competition you might have;

FACTOR   **Priority**
1. We DK if Sun Systems is planning to enter our market?   A

Action Steps	Who	Due date
1. Visit Sun System web site. R	RKS	09/15/03
2. Order Annual report / 10K / 10Q from Sun Systems.	JBS	09/15/03
3. Check analyst reports for industry trends.	JBS	09/20/03

> ** As you will notice, one factor can drive several action steps - or it can be a 1-to-1 ration - or a single action step may take care of several factors.

Once you have written all of the action steps necessary to handle the factors and achieve the objective - simply put them into date order - and you have a step-by-step Strategic Action Plan that is time bound and has specific individuals who have been assigned to take responsibility for every important item.

Note : remember to number all of your factors and action steps so that you can cross-reference them - ensuring that you don't let any fall through the cracks!

TASK 3 - STRATEGIC ACTION PLAN – WORKSHOP

List a major Strategic Business Objective - and the corresponding action steps (in date order) needed to achieve it – be sure to assign every action step to an individual who will be completely responsible for taking care of it – and also put a reference number back to the factor that this action is attached to from the plan to make sure you have created specific action steps to address every important factor. This is a bit redundant — but the finished action plan is sure to be precise, focused and clear.

Strategic Business Objective			
ACTION	Who	Date	Factor

CONTINGENCY PLANS

As you conduct your SWOT / Gap analysis there is a good chance that you will uncover specific factors that represent serious decision points for your organization (either positive or negative). It is crucial that you include these issues in the plan so that you and your team can anticipate them and manage them accordingly.

These factors may deal with issues such as:

New competitors entering the market.
New markets becoming available.
New regulation or deregulation in the industry.
Loss of a major competitor, customer, supplier.
New technology that makes some of your products or services obsolete.
Recession, war, natural disaster.
Loss of a key employee . loss of a facility.

The list could go on, but each of these subjects could seriously impact your business – and must be planned for. The suggested course of action is to create a series of contingency plans based on the probability and impact of a specific issue.

Probability: what is the likelihood that this factor will come to pass. You can score this either as a percentage of 100 – or Low, Medium, High.

Impact: if it were to happen — what would the potential impact be to your business — Low, Medium, High.

For example, you may know that one of your current competitors is struggling due to over-expansion and may have to close down some of their operations in your region. If that were to happen — it could be an excellent opportunity for you to secure their customers and gain significant market share. You might score that as:

Acme forced to close all Colorado stores — Probability: 70% / Impact: High

For all high probability/high impact issues, you and your team should create a set of contingency plans that can be implemented as soon as the issue reaches a certain *"**Trigger Point**"* - a set threshold event that will indicate it is time for you to take action. Once a trigger point has been reached — you will be able to implement your contingency plan swiftly - gaining superior advantage in the marketplace or reducing exposure.

SUMMARY

We have now completed the "planning" part of Strategic Planning - the last two tasks deal with implementation and evaluation (which should also be planned for!).

A broad overview of the process you have just completed looks like this:

Step 1: Define long-term direction of the company by asking yourself and your team: - "What is our business - what should it be – what will it be in 3-5 years?"

Step 2: Create a Vision Statement to clarify and communicate that direction.

Step 3: Scrutinize the current position of the company. - SWOT Analysis —— leading to GAP analysis

Step 4: Based on current position and analysis - undertake comprehensive factoring process.
- everything that could positively or negatively effect our ability to accomplish the vision.

Step 5: Make sure factors are clearly written,

numbered, specific statements of fact and then prioritize each (A,B,C) according to level of action required to address the issue.

Step 6: Group similar factors and number the factor groups.
Step 7: Based on Factor groupings, you should notice several common themes – which then become your broad Strategic Business Objectives (strategic thrusts).

Step 8: For each of your major strategic business objectives, develop specific action steps to address the objective and move the organization toward achieving the vision.

Step 9: Make sure the action steps are SMART - cross referenced to the factors - have a due date - and are assigned to a specific individual for implementation.

Step 10: Implement the Strategic Action Plan.

Step 11: Evaluate constantly - review/adjust/change as necessary.

Notes:

ABOUT THE AUTHOR

John Millar is the Managing Director, Senior Business Coach Trainer and Consultant with More Profit Less Time Pty Ltd and CEO-ONDEMAND. Along with his many other business interests, John is proud to have been an associate of the most successful coaching team in the world.

He is recognized as a global leader and has been benchmarked against over 1,300 colleagues in 31 countries. John has over 25 years of hands-on ownership, management, coaching, and entrepreneurial experience in a broad range of industry sectors, including retail, wholesale, import, export, IT, trades and trade services, automotive, primary production, food services, transport, manufacturing, mining, professional services, the fitness industry, and more.

He has extensive experience developing and providing training for small to medium-sized companies and a variety of publicly listed corporate companies.

John is an accomplished and talented public and professional speaker. He has been a mentor working with sales/management activities for businesses with a turnover under $100,000 per annum, over $100 million turnover, and everything in between, with great success.

John currently works with business owners and their teams across Australia and has a "Whatever it takes" attitude that has enabled him to help his clients grow their business profits by up to 800%.

If you are ready to be coached by one of the best in the business, register at:

www.ceo-ondemand.com.au

Make sure to visit www.moreprofitlesstime.com for the new online Management Development Program: The Business Essentials Series.

CEOONDEMAND

ACCLAIM FOR JOHN MILLAR'S

Business Coaching and Training in their own words...

"Without John Millar as my Business Coach I wouldn't have a business today."—Grant Jennings Managing Director, Jigsaw Projects

"Taking the decision to be coached and trained by John Millar was carefully considered after experiencing those who over promised and under delivered. I am pleased to say the content of his courses are the tools we all need to master as business owners. His delivery is engaging, thought provoking and empowering and after every session I came away re-energised. John always makes himself available for business building advice both via Skype and face to face beyond the scope of delivery. With his extensive personal experience in building small businesses, he knows and understands what it takes to establish and grow a business. I have no hesitation endorsing John Millar as an educator and business coach and the bonus is he is a very nice person."—Anne Lederman Managing Director FB Salons"

Johns training with my management team was excellent, it was very different from the business coaching and support I have had in the past. John was clear, thoughtful and he addressed the issues we needed to cover without us even knowing they were being addressed! His follow up has been fantastic and exactly what I needed. I would recommend John and his team to anyone looking at getting some business coaching and training done" —Wendy Crawford, Peopleworx

"In my dealings with John as our business coach, I have found him to be a motivated and insightful agent of positive change. He is able to burrow down to the root cause of issues and introduce effective forms of measurement. John then identifies and implements practical solutions and is there to provide the gentle persuasion required to ensure that results are achieved." —Mark Felton, Lindale Insurances

"You have coached and trained us so well throughout the year that we are now used to & find it easy to prepare a 90 day plan, then breaks it down to actionable bite size pieces. Planning in business & personal life certainly is important. It allows us to identify the important things & the bigger picture. Thank you for your support & guidance throughout the year. And not to mention your insight, external perspective to review & assist our business moving forward." —Linda Turner, Director Roy A McDonald Certified Practicing Accountants

"If you want to achieve sales results you never thought were possible and give yourself a competitive edge my strong suggestion is to engage John services and listen closely to what John has to say, during the time I was trained by John I was one of eight sales consultants in a national business for 10 out of the 13 months I lead the sales tally and in 1 quarter I generated three times the revenue of the national sales force combined. Johns training and experience was well worth the investment and paid big dividends. Thanks John." —Julian Fadini, Bellvue Capital

"John is a very enthusiastic trainer and business coach, he is very passionate about getting business owners and their team where they need to be. He goes the extra mile to keep ahead of the latest developments which he then uses to benefit his clients." —Darren Reddy CPA

"I have been to a few seminars and heard John speak numerous times about sales, marketing and business. He is a very knowledgeable and extremely enthusiastic business coach in all his interactions and I would recommend him to all business owners who need a sales and marketing boost!" —Andrew Heath, Managing Director, Fresh Living Group

"I worked with John Millar and found his business knowledge, passion and innovation to be inspiring. He has always been able to set (and achieve) strategic long and short-term goals both for himself and his clients without losing that personal connection he builds with everyone he meets. He has been and I believe will continue to be a strong mentor and trainer for anyone wanting to take that next step in their business." —Bree Webster, Online Marketing Guru

"Massive Action Day" – what an understatement, John Millars 4 hour frenzy challenged me to seriously review areas of my business I would not have gone to .... In this way, the process identified incongruence's in my mind, my business and my modus operandi. It's created a paradigm shift. Thanks John, the road map just got a whole lot clearer. Your friendship and insights since 2003 have been a gift to my business and I." —Andrew Reay, Counsellor, Hypnotherapist and Counsellor, Thinkshift Transformations

"John Millar is not your usual Business coach or trainer; he gets involved with you and your business and provides hands on help to make sure you follow through on his advice. He is highly motivated to help his clients and his personal guarantee certainly shows this. He has now transposed his thoughts, advice and love of good business onto a series of DVD's in his business venture – More Profit Less Time. This has excellent tips and advice for anyone either starting out or already in business. I highly recommend John to any business owner who wants to run a business and not a j.o.b.!" — Darren Cassidy, Managing Director HR2U

"I and many of my Business Partners and colleagues have worked with John since 2010 as our business oath, trainer and motivator and found him to be an extremely motivational person to assist us achieve our business goals. This company and its products allows for John's skill set to be accessed by a wider number of potential clients. His very professional DVD series is extremely good value for money and is easily accessible for all of us who are time poor. If you are looking to maximise your and your business's results and to start achieving your goals and dreams, contact John; you won't look back!!" —Mark Cleland, Mortgage Choice

"John develops real relationships with the people he comes into contact with. He is pasionate about what he does. His DVD and group training series, is full of good ideas and process to make your business better. Knowing what to do and actually doing it are two different things. John is excellent at helping you get things done." —Carey Rudd, Sales Director, Online Knowledge

"I have known John since 2004 and found him to be extremely knowledgably in both Sales and Business systems as a business coach without peer. John has provided me with business advice as well as personal coaching over the years, helping me with the running of my organisation. I'm impressed with John's DVD series where he has condensed a lot of the information in an easy to follow format that any business owner can use immediately. I wish he had released these DVDs earlier, as they are a goldmine of information, and practical how to that allow anyone to increase the profit in their business and get back valuable wasted time." —Steve Psaradellis, Managing Director, TEBA

"John's DVD and workbook delivery of his no-nonsense advice provides a low-cost option for those business owners looking to set and achieve goals that will increase profit. I found the conversational style of the DVD's easy to follow, whilst the requirement to pause the DVD and write down some action points ensured a level of commitment to the advice being provided." — Mark Felton, Lindale Insurances

"I only met John briefly at a BNI meeting and knew instantly i need to hire him for my business as my business coach. His attitude towards work and how to improve my cash line had an instant effect on before, even before I finally hired him on an official basis. I found myself thinking "what would John do" and this was only after just meeting him. I cannot see my business expend and give me "More Profit Less Time" without John's expert direction and training. If you want to succeed in business life, you need John Millar, without him you're just kidding yourself " —Leslie Cachia, Managing Director, Letac Drafting

"I can highly recommend John Millar to any business owner who wants to grow his business. When I hear very positive feedback from colleagues who are skeptics by nature about John's ability and skills, I know John will help all those he comes in contact with. John comes with a selfless nature and the willingness to work inside a client's business to make it succeed. Rare indeed!" — Darren Cassidy, Managing Director, HR2U"I first met John Millar in mid-2010 and have always found him to be of an honest and generous character that engenders an easy association with him. I love how easy he is to listen to and how passionate he is about his work and topics. John demonstrates a love for life and his work and I have no hesitation in recommending his services." —Kathie M Thomas, Managing Director, VA

"I have listened to John speak on a number of occasions

and find him a very knowledgeable speaker with a passion for what he does. I have also interacted with a number of his clients and they all tell me that he helps them achieve results in their business. If you are looking for business help John is a person you can trust." — Carey Rudd, Sales Director, Online Knowledge

"John knows his stuff, he knows how the get results, John has so many great ideas in building a business and helping business owners work less and make more money. John has released a DVD set on doing just that. I have watched the 1st one and it was great, very informative and easy to understand, I happily recommend John to anyone in need of help and guidance" —Frank Eramo, Proprietor, Dynotune

"I have known John only for a short time, however the impact that he has had on me, not just my business has helped me to visualise opportunities that I began to doubt my ability to realise. He is encouraging and at the same time challenging so that he can/you can, begin to see how to maximise the business potential, John calls it being an unreasonable friend, I call it being a mate. If you have any questions about the direction of your business, if you want to seem your bottom line improve not just turnover but real profit, if you want a person who will work with you then I strongly recommend that you engage him at your earliest convenience. John is the best thing that has happened to my business. I could tell you about the way he is on track to make 1/2 a million for me on his contacts alone, but that actually sells him short, he has become like my partner in business, and cares about my success as if it was his own, we will flourish because I took the step to employ his training to help me grow. If you get a chance to get him training you, don't wait like I did, get in as quickly as possible, his time is your business and if like me your business is to make money, then every day you don't have him on retainer you lose money." —Russell Summers, Managing Director, The Give Life Centre

"It's usually easy to be mediocre in business but it's impossible when you have John Millar training you. He has been my right hand since 2003!" —David Manser, CFO, Hydrosteer

"I now have a commercial, profitable business and now it's my choice when I work IN my business and when I work ON it and have had john helping me in business since 1988. I can't imagine not having John as a part of our business." —David Wall, Director, D&K Transport

"The work John has done since 2008 coaching and training our marketing team, administration and finance teams, buyers, store managers and staff nationally have been fantastic." —Ross Sudano, Director, Anaconda Adventure Stores

"John is a creative, professional, practical and committed business coach and trainer. His approach since we first met him in 1994 to working with a client team through the application of useful tools, information and anecdotes along with his easy going & easy to understand delivery sets him apart from other business coaches that I have used in the past." — Anthony Beasley, Director, The Astra Group

"I have worked with John Millar for the since 2004 and I

didn't think it was possible to achieve what we have achieved together. His business coaching, training and services just get better and better!" —Terrance Chong, Managing Director, Echo Graphics and Printing

"John's business coaching, training and support has transformed our business across Australia and New Zealand since 2008."—Rose Vis, Managing Director, VIP Australia

"We first met John in 2005, he is AMAZING at sales, marketing, operations, logistics, finance training and so much more. Since engaging John as our business coach our business has exploded, our team are happy, our clients are raving about us and my husband and I now take at least 12 weeks holidays a year, EVERY year." — Shirley Du, Director, Goldline Technology

"It's the no nonsense results driven business coaching and training focus John bought to the table that had such a massive effect on our business." —David Runkel, Director, Tracomp Fabrication and Steel

"We started working with John in early 2010, within 90 days of working with and being trained by John Millar we had the biggest and most profitable month in our 15 year history. That's impressive." —Hugh Gilchrist, Managing Director, Australian Moulding Company

"If you don't have John as your business trainer you aren't meeting your business potential." —Don Robertson, Director, Medallion Electrical Services.

www.ingramcontent.com/pod-product-compliance
Lightning Source LLC
Chambersburg PA
CBHW061200180526
45170CB00002B/888